Will
Over Water

How the Red River region rallied to fight the flood of 2009

PUBLISHED BY THE FORUM OF FARGO-MOORHEAD

WDAY FLOOD DVD INSIDE

CAROLYN KASTER / THE ASSOCIATED PRESS

FROST-COVERED HOMES AND TREES are surrounded by floodwaters as the Red River crests March 28, 2009, in Fargo.

Copyright © 2009
The Forum of Fargo-Moorhead

The Forum of Fargo-Moorhead
101 N. 5th St.
Fargo, ND 58102

PO Box 2020
Fargo, ND 58107

WDAY Television
301 8th St. N.
Fargo, ND 58102

Web sites: www.inforum.com, www.wday.com

Printed by:
Forum Communications Printing
4601 16th Ave. N.
Fargo, ND 58102

Cover images: Copyright © The Forum
Photo by Dave Wallis / The Forum

ISBN: 978-0-615-29953-2

To order additional copies of this book, contact The Forum at the above address, or call (701) 235-7311.

Reporting by: The Forum staff
Photography provided by: Forum Communications, The Associated Press, Star Tribune
River level sourcing: USGS

Printed in the United States of America

VOLUNTEERS USE SANDBAGS to plug a culvert in the Oak Creek neighborhood of Fargo.

DAVE WALLIS / THE FORUM

TABLE OF CONTENTS

FROM THE PUBLISHER

THE BOOK'S COVER PHOTO of Zach Boor says it all. On March 23, in the runup to the biggest flood this region's ever seen, the 12-year-old Fargo boy was excused from classes at Discovery Middle School so he could join thousands of other area volunteers in building dikes that would protect Fargo-Moorhead and the region.

One by one, these volunteers toiled in the snow, mud and muck, filling and then relaying sandbags down long lines of human chains that built the levees ever higher as crest predictions seemed to rise by the day.

Besides the volunteers, those who belong to the National Guard, law enforcement agencies, fire departments and other safety responders and public officials went beyond the call of duty.

The people were exhausted, but they laughed. They were dirty, but they smiled. They were concerned, but determined. They thought: If anybody can beat Mother Nature, we in the Red River region can.

So doctors and lawyers joined alongside convicts and students in sandbag lines. This was about community. This was about saving our communities. A collective purpose brought the region together like never before. And the world watched in amazement. They were inspired by the sense of community, the heroics of people banding together in huge numbers to save perhaps the one and only thing they have in common: their place in the world.

The Forum, inforum.com and WDAY-TV and radio couldn't let this significant chapter in our region's history pass without chronicling it in some significant way.

"Will Over Water" is a testament to our region's fortitude and determination to fight back the flood of 2009.

Let's face it: We're proud of our great accomplishment. We should be.

This book is dedicated to everyone who, like 12-year-old Zach Boor, had a hand in making us stand a little taller today.

William C. Marcil

William C. Marcil
Publisher of The Forum of Fargo-Moorhead
CEO of Forum Communications Co.

PROLOGUE

THE SANDBAGS ARE GONE, and the riverbanks are dry.

The once-unruly Red no longer poses an imminent threat.

People have resumed their daily lives: They're back at work, back to enjoying time with their families, and back to planning for the future.

It's hard to believe that just a short time ago we were in a full-blown fight to save our cities and homes from the ferocious floodwaters.

Yes, the spring 2009 flood was like nothing we had seen before.

Though the numbers continue to evolve, an estimated 100 to 150 Cass County homes sustained some water damage during the flood, with up to 20 percent having main floor damage.

In Clay County, roughly 70 homes ended up with major water damage, while 300 to 400 had some damage.

Many of those people are still picking up the pieces and will be for years to come, as talk shifts to buyouts and permanent flood control.

And yet, it could have been much worse. After all, our cities were largely unharmed.

Few would argue that the credit for that success goes to the tens of thousands of volunteers who threw their hearts, bodies and souls into fighting back the floodwaters.

They came together from every age group and every walk of life. It didn't matter. They shared one common goal: to keep the cities safe and dry.

It was all the motivation they needed.

It was will over water.

DOWNTOWN FARGO is seen as the Red River continues to rise on March 28.

CAROLYN KASTER
ASSOCIATED PRESS

CHAPTER 1: A LONG, HARD WINTER

THERE WERE SIGNS. The record December snowfall was among the first. That might have been OK had it not been for the deluge of fall rain that came before it. The soil was saturated; the ditches and culverts bloated with frozen water.

Then came more than 24 inches of snow. And it wasn't even January.

By late February, forecasters were predicting a 60 percent chance of the Red River rising above 35.1 feet – major flood stage is 30 feet – and a 10 percent chance of it surpassing 38.5 feet – just shy of the 1997 crest.

The final blow: A March 10 snowstorm that forced the Fargo-Moorhead area into standstill mode, dumping more than 10 inches of snow.

The ground was soaked, and another weather system was headed our way.

Then, on March 19, Fargo-Moorhead got the bad news: The cities had roughly a week to prepare for a flood that could reach 1997 proportions.

TOM AND TANYA LEIFERMAN'S dog eats the snow they are cleaning from their driveway March 11, 2009, in Jamestown, N.D., after a two-day blizzard left several inches of snow.

JOHN M. STEINER
THE JAMESTOWN SUN

FACING PAGE: Steve Savageau shovels out his vehicles March 11, 2009, at his home on Gibraltor Avenue North in Fargo.

MICHAEL VOSBURG
THE FORUM

FRIDAY, MARCH 20

THE RED RIVER was officially above flood stage – 18 feet – and sandbagging efforts began to ramp up.

The mission: to fill 2 million sandbags to protect Fargo and Cass County from the Red, now expected to crest between 37 and 40 feet between March 28 and April 4.

Work already was under way on emergency dikes around downtown Fargo's City Hall, and residents of Oakport Township north of Moorhead were busily sandbagging their homes, hoping to avoid another disaster like 1997.

The biggest challenge was finding enough volunteers to get the jobs done. After all, thousands of students and other would-be volunteers were in Minneapolis, cheering on the Bison men's basketball team's debut at The Big Dance.

Meanwhile, Moorhead Mayor Mark Voxland also urged residents to sandbag, fearing 600 to 700 houses could be affected if the river got as high as predicted.

VOLUNTEERS fill the Fargo City Garage to man octopus machines purchased to mass produce sandbags at what became known as "Sandbag Central."

MICHAEL VOSBURG
THE FORUM

FARGO WATER DEPARTMENT workers Mike Kramer, front left, and Cordell Roemmich, right, help co-workers install a flood gate northeast of the Oak Grove School campus. The flood wall was designed to protect the campus and surrounding neighborhood to a flood depth of 41 feet.

MICHAEL VOSBURG
THE FORUM

MIKE SCHULTZ, a surveyor for the city of Fargo, marks the height a 41-foot flood would reach on Oak Street. That levee protection height would later be raised.

MICHAEL VOSBURG / THE FORUM

A LONG, HARD WINTER

A RIBBON OF ICE shows the normal channel of the Red River as it remains mostly intact between Fargo and Wahpeton, N.D. Water from melting snow pools in the oxbow loops of the river as the edges of the ice start to break apart.

DAVE WALLIS / THE FORUM

VOLUNTEERS use shovels to keep sand moving into funnels to fill sandbags at Fargo's Sandbag Central.

DAVE WALLIS
THE FORUM

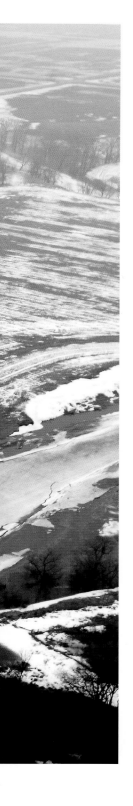

SATURDAY, MARCH 21

FLOODING WAS no longer far from anyone's mind.

The Red was swelling, and overland flooding already plagued the southern end of the Valley. Richland and Wilkin counties scrambled to keep up.

Fargo-Moorhead residents were starting to get a sense of what was coming.

The mood was shifting from calm to concerned.

And then there was the weather.

A powerful storm system was on its way and was expected to drop up to 2 inches of rain, followed by snow.

It was a race against time and Mother Nature.

JIM O'MEARA of Northern Improvement walks the dike on Second Street North in Fargo to survey the height between the Red River and Fargo City Hall.

DAVE WALLIS
THE FORUM

SUNDAY, MARCH 22

ANY LINGERING DOUBTS about this flood's fury were cast aside.

It was the news no one wanted to hear: The Red River flood crest was now expected to be between 39 and 41 feet – a foot higher than anyone thought.

Equally worrisome: The crest would likely arrive by week's end, a day earlier than originally thought.

Things had gone from bad to worse.

More than 200 National Guard soldiers and airmen joined volunteers at "Sandbag Central."

Schools canceled classes.

Media outlets began delivering news around the clock.

An urgent appeal went out for sandbaggers.

But would it be enough?

MINNESOTA NATIONAL GUARD MEMBERS and Moorhead police patrol the intersection of Fifth Street and 30th Avenue South to keep sightseers out of the way so trucks can get to their destinations. These checkpoints were set up all along the river.

CARRIE SNYDER
THE FORUM

RED RIVER

THE RED RIVER starts to touch the bottom of the already closed Broadway bridge in north Fargo.

CARRIE SNYDER / THE FORUM

GERAD FUGLEBERG, from left, grabs a bag while Zach Ficenec, Chris Czichotzki and Luke Paper fill the bags with sand on Chrisan Way near 76th Avenue South in Fargo. The group planned to fill 1,000 sandbags to help protect Ficenec's house.

MICHAEL VOSBURG
THE FORUM

FLOOD PROFILE

SARA LEPP

DIRECTOR, FIRSTLINK VOLUNTEER CENTER

BY KELLY SMITH / THE FORUM

MICHAEL VOSBURG / THE FORUM

It wasn't exactly what Lepp signed on to do when she "just fell into" the position three years ago.

"You just kind of take it as it comes," she said, clutching her cell phone and a Diet Coke between numerous phone calls with city officials, the Federal Emergency Management Agency and media. "I was overseeing kind of everything."

During the flood of 2009, Lepp orchestrated more than 100,000 sandbag volunteers. They're the volunteers who became the face nationally of Fargo's massive effort to save the city.

Lepp also coordinated volunteers who staffed the flood hot line that the community relied on for 24/7 information.

"She may not have been in the spotlight, but she created the framework for what that spotlight was," Cwiak said. "What was the biggest part of the flood fight? It was the volunteers. Who built that? Sara Lepp and FirstLink."

Lepp worked with volunteers from the American Red Cross, the Salvation Army and AmeriCorps and was in close contact with Fargo, Moorhead, Clay County, Cass County and FEMA officials.

She also worked with the 75-some North Dakota

S ARA LEPP was an unlikely leader of the Red River Valley flood fight. Just three years into her first job out of college, the young woman unaccustomed to the public limelight quickly turned into the "go-to person" for the flood-fight volunteer efforts.

As the director of FirstLink's volunteer center, the 26-year-old Lepp was a leader among a group of mostly middle-aged men.

"She's the unsung hero of the flood," said Carol Cwiak, who worked with Lepp coordinating volunteers at the temporary call center. "She should run for office next."

State University emergency management students whom Cwiak teaches.

But Lepp, an unassuming leader, deflects any questions over the enormous task she faced.

"It's one of those things you don't expect to be in," she said. "I don't think about it. You do what's needed."

Sporting a blazer and pants, the tall woman with short blond hair shrugs at how she managed it all.

"I haven't really put a whole lot of thought in it," she said. "At times, it was a little surreal. You kind of just go with it. You're just one piece of the team, the puzzle."

At the height of the flood fight, the volunteer call center became Lepp's home.

"I just felt bad leaving," she said.

So, she worked 12- to 18-hour days.

"The phones were so busy, we couldn't even pick up the phone to dial out," said Tasha Conway, the director of the organization's hot line operations. "You name it, we've answered it."

When Lepp wasn't at the call center, she was trekking between the six volunteer sites, checking to make sure they had enough food, buses and volunteers.

"It's not an easy job by any means," said Cass County

Emergency Manager Dave Rogness. "I've held her feet to the fire on a couple occasions. And she's done very well."

What she did during the flood

wasn't necessarily in the job description either.

"The job has definitely grown," said FirstLink Executive Director Cindy Miller. "She did an amazing job organizing it all."

FirstLink, a nonprofit organization once a part of United Way, has numerous community resource programs from emergency preparedness training to a suicide hot line.

The organization, with only four full-time employees, is contracted by area cities and counties to coordinate volunteer efforts for the region's major disasters.

Lepp first heard of FirstLink as a college student studying child development at North Dakota State University. There, she got an internship at FirstLink, graduated in 2005 and, by 2006, she was the director of the volunteer center.

"This came up, and I haven't

left yet," said the Fergus Falls, Minn., native. "It's not something you wake up and say, 'I want to be a volunteer coordinator.' It's a cool job; it was

---

"IT'S ONE OF THOSE THINGS YOU DON'T EXPECT TO BE IN. I DON'T THINK ABOUT IT. YOU DO WHAT'S NEEDED."
— SARA LEPP

---

just something I don't think I knew existed."

Now, she's getting back to what she did before the flood – "it's kind of random, like, depends on the day," she said about her normal responsibilities.

For Lepp, it has all been a learning experience. After all, she didn't have an emergency management background and, unlike other community leaders who can draw on past experience, was in ninth grade during the '97 flood.

Yet, her youth and inexperience wasn't a concern for those who worked closely with her.

"If someone is going to judge Sara Lepp because she is young and inexperienced, they've really made an incorrect assumption," Cwiak said. "She really managed this event with grace and professionalism. I would challenge anyone to do a better job."

WINTER 2009

CHAPTER 2: HEADED FOR BATTLE

"FEAR IS SETTING IN. WE'RE SEEING THAT ON THE STREETS."
- FARGO SALVATION ARMY CAPT. ADAM MOORE

VOLUNTEERS WORK WITH SANDBAGS to protect the Applecourt senior citizens housing unit in Breckenridge, Minn. An unexpected dip in the Red River miles upstream cheered sandbaggers struggling to raise this city's protective dikes high enough to withstand possible record flooding. The National Weather Service lowered its crest forecast for Wahpeton and its cross-river neighbor, Breckenridge, to 18 feet by the next morning, well below the tops of their dikes.

RICHARD SENNOTT / THE MINNEAPOLIS STAR TRIBUNE

HEADED FOR BATTLE

PATRICK STOA, left, catches a sandbag tossed to him by Geoffrey Billingsley as they, along with many other volunteers, construct a dike along the north side of Rose Coulee in Fargo's Rose Creek neighborhood. Stoa, a student at Minnesota State University Moorhead, and Billingsley, a student at the University of North Dakota, worked in front of the home of Mary Unhjem.

DAVE WALLIS / THE FORUM

MONDAY, MARCH 23

BRACE YOURSELF.

That was the message from city leaders. Fargo-Moorhead residents weren't backing down. They heard the message loud and clear and sprung into action.

More than 10,000 people turned out to help combat the floodwaters on this dreary day. Buses could barely keep up with all the people who wanted to be shuttled to sandbag sites to lend a helping hand.

But people were hungry for information, too. Everyone had the same questions. Will my home be safe? Can we save the city? Will it be as bad – or worse – than 1997?

City and township officials from throughout the area set up neighborhood and community meetings, hoping to ease some concerns.

THIS ELECTRONIC BILLBOARD on Fargo's 32nd Avenue South west of 25th Street had three different messages encouraging people to help fight the flood.

MICHAEL VOSBURG
THE FORUM

TUESDAY, MARCH 24

THE WINDOW OF OPPORTUNITY

for the cities to build strong dikes was small, but city and county leaders were confident it could be done.

The big push was under way.

Colder temperatures were expected to set in overnight. People worried the weather could create problems for placing sandbags. Then again, the cold could slow the flow of the spring melt and the rise of the Red.

Still, people needed to be prepared for the worst. Talk shifted to evacuation plans.

For residents in some parts of the Valley, it was already a reality. In Crookston, Minn., many began fleeing their homes after the Red Lake River surged almost 4 feet in just a few hours.

TYLER NESS helps load a friend's belongings for evacuation from Crookston, Minn. The Red Lake River behind the property was expected to crest at 26.4 feet the next day.

MICHAEL VOSBURG
THE FORUM

VOLUNTEERS HELP place sandbags outside the home of Jeremy Kuipers in Kragnes, Minn. The home was built in 1902.

RICHARD TSONG-TAATARII / THE MINNEAPOLIS STAR TRIBUNE

VOLUNTEERS WORK in mud as they form a line to pass sandbags to protect a north Fargo neighborhood.

DAVE WALLIS / THE FORUM

ONE OF DOUG STENSGARD'S DOGS, Annie, looks out over what used to be a 5-acre yard and an outbuilding now flooded by the rising Red River south of Fargo. Stensgard built an earthen and sandbag dike around his home.

CAROLYN KASTER / THE ASSOCIATED PRESS

ISABEL KALLMEYER, 9, works with her neighbor Caitlin Carson, 6, to fill sandbags that will be piled around the Kallmeyer home in Fargo.

CAROLYN KASTER
THE ASSOCIATED PRESS

CARRIE SNYDER / THE FORUM

VOLUNTEERS BUILD A WALL OF SANDBAGS along the amphitheater at Trollwood Performing Arts School in south Moorhead. The sandbags were being built up 2 feet tall to help protect under the stage area where equipment is stored. The school was moved from its location in north Fargo to south Moorhead to protect it from the Red River. Landscaping was supposed to give further protection from the river, but the wet fall prevented its completion. Volunteers hoped it would be the only year they would have to sandbag at the new location.

HEADED FOR BATTLE

WEDNESDAY, MARCH 25

WE WERE IN "uncharted territory," Fargo's mayor declared as he opened the morning flood meeting that by now had become part of the daily routine.

It wasn't just the Red. The Wild Rice and Sheyenne rivers were becoming equally unwieldy.

In Cass County communities like Oxbow, Abercrombie and Hickson, a handful of residents began evacuating their homes, forcing boat rescues of at least 20 people.

In Clay County's Oakport Township and Georgetown, Minn., officials urged those with young and vulnerable individuals to move to safe havens.

And move they did. One by one, boat by boat.

DANNY McDORMAND of the U.S. Coast Guard signals to his team that there are two people who need to be rescued from the flooded home of Dick Huntley on Pfiffer Drive in Hickson, N.D.

CAROLYN KASTER
THE ASSOCIATED PRESS

VOLUNTEERS BUILD A DIKE of sandbags as high as 7 feet as snow falls along a creek on the west side of the Oak Creek neighborhood in south Fargo.

DAVE WALLIS / THE FORUM

DALE CARDWELL, left, and Jack Lubka struggle to push a boat free of ice in floodwaters of the Red River in Fargo.
CAROLYN KASTER
THE ASSOCIATED PRESS

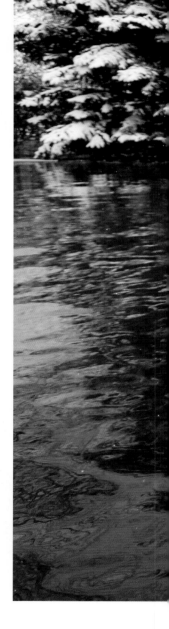

MICHAEL VOSBURG / THE FORUM

PAYLOADERS, trucks and airboats share the street in Oxbow, N.D.

HERB READ, left, and his son Tom Read look out over the flooded Red River as it rises up against sandbags that protect their home in Hickson, N.D. They refused evacuation by the U.S. Coast Guard.

CAROLYN KASTER / THE ASSOCIATED PRESS

A NATIONAL GUARD helicopter lands demolition crews on the Missouri River near Bismarck to blast a huge ice jam in a bid to open a channel, like pulling a giant plug to drain the flood threatening the city.

TOM STROMME
THE BISMARCK TRIBUNE

THURSDAY, MARCH 26

AREA RESIDENTS GOT the worst news possible: The Red River could reach a record 42 or 43 feet by the weekend. And the water might stay that high for seven days.

Never before had anyone seen a flood of such magnitude.

Both Fargo and Moorhead urged evacuations for several neighborhoods and, in an unprecedented move, patients were evacuated from all Fargo MeritCare hospitals as a precaution.

Residents throughout the area braced for the possibility of more evacuations.

But Fargo Mayor Dennis Walaker wasn't giving up: "We want to go down swinging if we go down."

TRAFFIC MOVES at a start-and-stop crawl along eastbound Interstate 94 near 17th Street South in Fargo. It was backed up from Interstate 29 into Moorhead as crews built levees around part of the Interstate 94 interchange at Moorhead's Eighth Street South.
MICHAEL VOSBURG
THE FORUM

OAK GROVE NEIGHBORHOOD RESIDENTS listen to information from city officials during a flood meeting at Oak Grove school.

DAVID SAMSON / THE FORUM

FARGO MAYOR DENNIS WALAKER, right, meets with members of the local and national media during a press conference at City Hall.

DAVID SAMSON
THE FORUM

JERRY FAROL, left, and his son, Scott, carry some of their possesions after getting off airboats as they were evacuated from their flooded home in the Heritage Hills area south of Fargo.

DAVE WALLIS / THE FORUM

A RESIDENT AND TWO VOLUNTEERS get a lift out of Briarwood south of Fargo.

MICHAEL VOSBURG / THE FORUM

DOLLY BEAUCAGE, 98, prays the rosary in her room as she prepares to evacuate with the rest of the residents at the Elim Rehab & Care Center in Fargo as the Red River continues to rise.

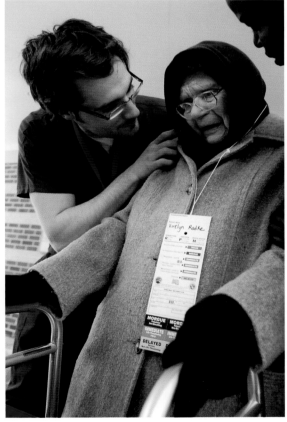

EVELYN RADKE is comforted by caregivers as she leaves with the rest of the residents at the Elim Rehab & Care Center in Fargo. North Dakota's largest city moves to the brink of potentially disastrous flooding as officials predict the Red River would reach a record-high crest of 41 feet.

HEADED TO BATTLE

FRIDAY, MARCH 27

THE RED RIVER made history, nudging past its 112-year-old record crest of 40.1 feet.

Flood-fighting efforts continued, but the streets around town grew eerily still.

The North Dakota National Guard took command of several major thoroughfares, giving trucks faster access to areas in need of dikes and sandbags.

Fargo and Moorhead schools took a bold step and canceled classes for the entire next week, and evacuees began trickling into shelters set up around the area.

Meanwhile, volunteers and emergency jump teams continued to battle levee leaks and river breakouts.

Flood watch was in full throttle.

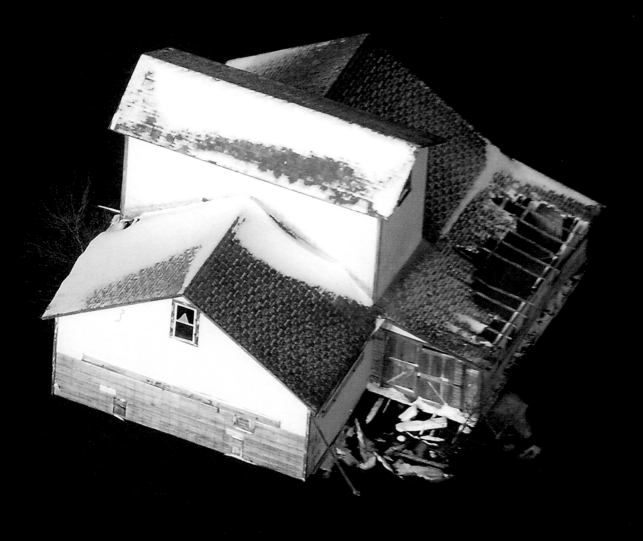

AN ISOLATED HOME in Red River floodwaters is shown in this aerial photo taken near Fargo.

VOLUNTEERS from Valley Water Rescue watch a home burn in Oakport Township, just north of Moorhead. The home, which was sandbagged but surrounded by floodwaters, had been evacuated earlier by the residents. Fire crews couldn't get closer than 200 feet from the home because the area around it was flooded.

CHRIS POLYDOROFF / THE PIONEER PRESS

JEREMY SERGEY, right, and Dan Farley, left, of the U.S. Coast Guard, pilot their airboat to shore with evacuees in Briarwood as the Red River continues to rise.

CAROLYN KASTER
THE ASSOCIATED PRESS

HELEN FOSS is helped off a U.S. Coast Guard airboat after being rescued from her flooded home in Briarwood.

CAROLYN KASTER
THE ASSOCIATED PRESS

VOLUNTEERS FILL SANDBAGS around the clock at a frantic pace at the Fargodome. The dome floor became ground zero for sandbagging operations during the height of flooding.

DAVID SAMSON / THE FORUM

A WORKER LEVELS sand on Hesco Concertainer basket dike down the middle of Harwood Drive in south Fargo as the Red River continues to rise.

CAROLYN KASTER
THE ASSOCIATED PRESS

FLOODWATERS of the Red River lap at the Main Avenue Bridge between Fargo, on the left, and Moorhead.

SNOW FLURRIES fall as scores of volunteers build up a dike to hold back the rising Red River in Fargo. Thousands of shivering, tired residents got out while they could and others prayed that miles of sandbagged levees would hold as the surging Red River threatened to unleash the biggest flood North Dakota's largest city had ever seen.

CLOCKWISE FROM LEFT, Kathy Anderson, Jillain Ehnert, Delene Gunderson and Sarah Harper work on filling sandbags at the new Trollwood Performing Arts School in south Moorhead.

CARRIE SNYDER / THE FORUM

CONCORDIA STUDENTS
Amy Luther, from left, Amy Freeman, Kelly Kalvoda and Andrea Rognlien fill sandbags in the Fargodome.

MICHAEL VOSBURG
THE FORUM

STUDENTS SAVE THE DAY

LOOKING DOWN THE ROWS of sandbag volunteers, shivering and muddy, each face told a different story.

But many had one thing in common: They were students.

High school and college students came out in force when the calls went out for volunteers. Classes around the area had been canceled, and the area youth were up for the challenge.

Most officials say the region's flood fight may not have been won without help from students.

NORTH DAKOTA STATE UNIVERSITY students wait for up to an hour outside the Memorial Union to volunteer to fill sandbags and build dikes.

MICHAEL VOSBURG / THE FORUM

FLOOD PROFILE

DENNIS WALAKER

MAYOR, FARGO

BY MILA KOUMPILOVA / THE FORUM

DAVE WALLIS / THE FORUM

DENNIS WALAKER was driving south of Fargo, sizing up the advance of floodwater toward his city, when the dreaded call came in from the National Weather Service.

The Fargo mayor's voice – the soft mutter that had soothed a stream of callers earlier that day – shot up. His weary face turned red.

"Forty-one to 43 feet?" he said, incredulous at a new, more pessimistic crest forecast. "Come on

guys, that can't be happening to us. We can't keep talking about these ranges because people are getting damn tired. What are we supposed to tell them?"

He was in his uncluttered GMC SUV along Cass County Road 17. It was March 26. Floodwaters had claimed the same road in 1997, when Walaker was Fargo's operations director and front-line fighter against a flood that devastated Grand Forks but left Fargo mostly unscathed. Just before the call came, the sight of the road jutting above frozen fields reassured him he was poised to win this latest standoff with the Red River.

For Walaker, the outburst was unexpected. More often, the straight-shooting mayor projected calm as the face of Fargo's flood fight.

Walaker had gotten bad news the day before as well when the weather service revised the crest projection to just over 41 feet.

"Your mind doesn't want to deal with it," said Walaker, who was elected mayor in 2006 after 32 years of working for the city. "Your mind wants to tell you it's impossible. But you don't have any choice."

Back in 1997, he would have taken a lonesome drive out through lakes country to clear his head. But back then, the city had a month, not days, to prepare. He had no time for such a luxury during this flood fight.

Just before 11 the night before, he finally got away from the meetings and media interviews and drove south of town to Hickson, where he could "feel what's going on." But at Old Highway 81, surging floodwaters blocked his way.

He was in what his wife, Mary, calls "flood mode," an ultra-focused, determined state when Walaker, 68, can function on four or five hours of sleep.

"The flood is a driving force to him," she said. "It's something he feels very deeply about."

Being a flood-fight spokesman rather than what former Fargo Mayor Bruce Furness, Walaker's 1997 boss, calls a "colonel in the cavalry" was an adjustment for Walaker. He missed being out by the dikes, where, according to Furness, Walaker spent 90 percent of his time in 1997, only popping in at City Hall to deliver updates in his mudcaked waders.

Mary Walaker, a retired teacher, recalls him sleeping at the city's sandbagging headquarters for a couple of weeks back then.

"I enjoyed the other role much better because I got out there to see if things got done," Dennis Walaker said. "It's hard to remove yourself from trying to make every decision."

On the afternoon of March 26, Walaker continued to make the rounds after a morning filled with news conferences and neighborhood meetings. His dark red Motorola phone rang every few minutes, and, from the passenger seat, he ladled out optimism and caution in equal measure. Lance Gaebe, Gov. John Hoeven's deputy chief of staff,

> *"THE FLOOD IS A DRIVING FORCE TO HIM. IT'S SOMETHING HE FEELS VERY DEEPLY ABOUT."*
> *– MARY WALAKER*

had volunteered to drive him after Walaker had trouble finding his car keys that morning.

When they crossed an icy, swollen Drain 27 on 45th Street South, Walaker muttered to himself "Oh God" a few times. But at a neighborhood meeting that day at Discovery School, he summoned a confident tone, telling residents the city's odds of winning were 3 or 4 to 1, "good at every horse parlor in the United States."

The night before, he told them if the city was successful in warding off the flood, he'd buy everyone a beer.

Walaker's off-hand manner in the spotlight – the fiddling with his glasses, the quips, the open "ho-ho-ho" laugh – is reassuringly unrehearsed.

He's the ultimate anti-politician. He's the face of the 2009 flood.

CHAPTER 3: WAITING, HOPING, PRAYING

WATER SPRAYS UP at volunteer firefighters from three neighboring towns as they attempt to pump Red River floodwaters out of George Korsmo's basement and brick-enclosed outdoor hot tub area in Moorhead.

CHARLES REX ARBOGAST
THE ASSOCIATED PRESS

DANIEL FRITH, right, leads volunteer firefighters from three neighboring towns and relatives in pushing water out of his uncle's Moorhead basement.

CHARLES REX ARBOGAST
THE ASSOCIATED PRESS

AN AMERICAN FLAG is surrounded by floodwaters along River Drive in south Moorhead.

DAVID SAMSON / THE FORUM

SATURDAY, MARCH 28

RESIDENTS WERE holding steady, breathing a collective sigh of relief upon hearing news that the Red River may have crested at 40.82 feet – a record.

But this was no time to declare victory. Residents had to stay on high alert, even though fatigue was beginning to set in.

This flood wasn't over. In fact, the National Weather Service was now forecasting a storm that could dump up to 8 inches of snow in the Wild Rice and Red river basins in the coming week.

That and the snowmelt in the southern end of the Valley still had to make its way north.

RED CROSS TRAINER MICHELE MILLER of Toledo, Ohio, works from the Veterans Memorial Arena in West Fargo. It had been their base of operations for what the Red Cross named DR419-09 ND-Flood.

CARRIE SNYDER
THE FORUM

NATIONAL GUARD PERSONNEL
walk in icy floodwaters near Fargo as they try
to rescue residents.

CAROLYN KASTER / THE ASSOCIATED PRESS

JIM AND BONNIE MYERS
were evacuated with little more than their dogs, Charlie and Shitara. The next day, their Oakport home was destroyed by fire.

SHERRI RICHARDS
THE FORUM

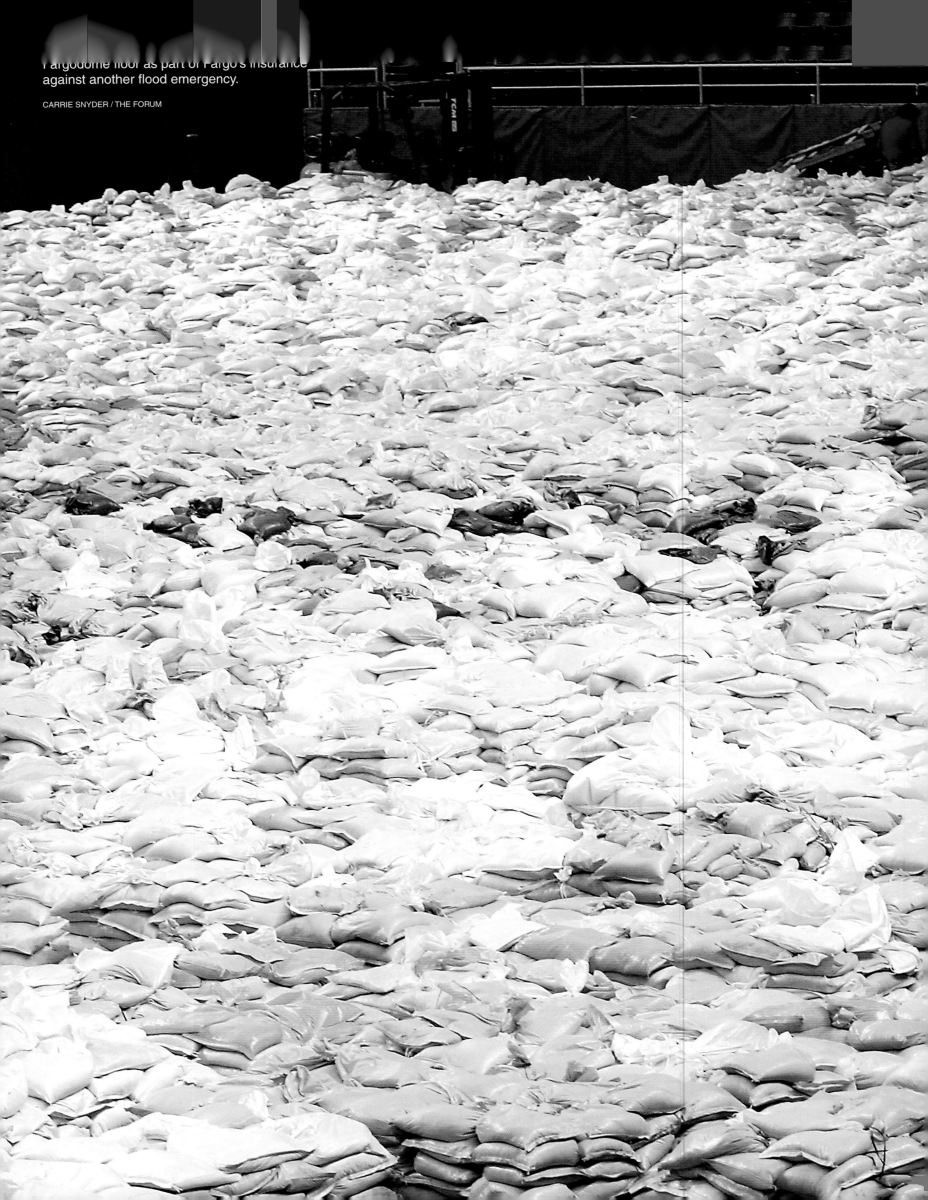

Fargodome floor as part of Fargo's insurance against another flood emergency.

DIKES HOLD BACK FLOODWATERS
as the Red River crests in Fargo-Moorhead.

CAROLYN KASTER / THE ASSOCIATED PRESS

THIS SANDBAGGING STATION in north Fargo sits quiet as the city shifts from building dikes to watching them.

MICHAEL VOSBURG
THE FORUM

A WORKER WALKS on a railroad bridge and over what is usually an underpass for traffic Saturday, March 28, in Moorhead. The Red River crested Saturday, forecasters said, leaving residents to wearily hope their sandbag-fortified dikes continue to hold back record-setting floodwaters.

ELAINE THOMPSON / THE ASSOCIATED PRESS

FLOODWATERS ENCIRCLE the
amphitheater at the new Trollwood Performing
Arts School location in south Moorhead.

DAVID SAMSON / THE FORUM

STREET SIGNS
are nearly submerged
in the Red River near
downtown Moorhead.

JIM MONE
THE ASSOCIATED PRESS

THE RESIDENCE of Daryl and Debbie
Helbling on El Cano Drive in south Fargo
is inundated with frozen floodwaters.

DAVID SAMSON / THE FORUM

AUSTEN NORMAN,
12, checks the level of
floodwaters in his
family's home in the
1900 block of 54th
Avenue North in
Oakport Township.

MICHAEL VOSBURG
THE FORUM

SUNDAY, MARCH 29

IT WAS A WAKE-UP CALL. The breach of a permanent flood wall at Fargo's Oak Grove Lutheran School overnight caught everyone's attention after a relatively quiet day.

Two of the five buildings on campus had water in them, and workers spent the day trying to seal off the leak and pump water out of the buildings.

But Sunday also was a day of reflection for many. People from all faiths came together to worship and to pray for strength.

Some rejoiced for the blessing of being largely spared thus far. For others, the burdens of the past week were too heavy.

But after the tough fight, there was starting to be reason for hope.

WORKERS SCRAMBLE to pull an outlet hose for a pump over a dike. A helicopter behind lowers a giant sandbag in an attempt to plug a leak at the flooded Oak Grove Lutheran School. Crews managed to largely contain the flooding to the school campus, preventing more widespread damage in nearby areas.

ELAINE THOMPSON
THE ASSOCIATED PRESS

A NATIONAL GUARD HELICOPTER lowers a large sandbag behind the flooded Oak Grove Lutheran School in an effort to stem flooding there.

ELAINE THOMPSON / THE ASSOCIATED PRESS

PEOPLE WORK to vacuum water out of a building at Oak Grove Lutheran School.

ELAINE THOMPSON
THE ASSOCIATED PRESS

"IF THERE'S EVER A TIME GOD'S PEOPLE
NEED TO BE PRAYING, THIS IS THE TIME."
– THE REV. VERN BAARDSON, TRIUMPH WEST COMMUNITY CHURCH

**MEMBERS OF THE FIRST ASSEMBLY
OF GOD** church in Fargo pray for people who
have been affected by Red River flooding.

CHARLES REX ARBOGAST / THE ASSOCIATED PRESS

MANDY JOHNSON of Fargo throws her hands up in praise while singing "Shout to the Lord" during the citywide worship service held by Triumph West Community Church at The Ramada Plaza Suites in Fargo.

A PARISHIONER folds his hands in prayer for victims of the Red River flooding during a citywide worship service at The Ramada Plaza Suites.

THE RED RIVER FLOODING is reflected in the visor of Sgt. 1st Class Todd Sudheimer, with the Minnesota National Guard based in St. Paul, as he looks out of his UH-60 Blackhawk helicopter south of Fargo.

CHARLES REX ARBOGAST / THE ASSOCIATED PRESS

VOLUNTEERS work six rows deep while filling sandbags in the Fargodome. The city reopened the operation to build up a reserve supply of filled sandbags.

DAVE WALLIS
THE FORUM

A CAT LOOKS OUT of its cage at an improvised animal shelter in West Fargo for pets displaced by area flooding. About 200 animals were brought to the site at the Red River Valley Fairgrounds, including about 150 dogs and cats and at least 37 horses. The site was also the new home to a goat, mule, donkey and two potbellied pigs.

ELAINE THOMPSON
THE ASSOCIATED PRESS

U.S. GEOLOGICAL SURVEY HYDROLOGIST JOEL GALLOWAY
pilots a small boat past flooded homes in Moorhead. Weary residents
welcomed the Red River's further retreat but faced an approaching
snowstorm expected to kick up wind-whipped waves that could threaten
the sandbag levees they built to protect the city from a major flood.

ELAINE THOMPSON / THE ASSOCIATED PRESS

MONDAY, MARCH 30

JUST WHEN IT SEEMED like winter might be waning, another storm howled in.

There were concerns of how the raging winds might rattle the sandbag levees that now lined the rivers.

Residents were urged to stay home. It was the right thing to do, but it was also starting to take its toll on area businesses.

Still, everyone was in the same boat.

And so residents continued to stay vigilant.

They waited. They watched. They continued to pray.

A STOP SIGN provides the only color as the Red River floods the area around the Moorhead Center Mall parking ramp.

DAVE WALLIS
THE FORUM

A SEMI-TRUCK AND TRAILER drives on Interstate 29 north of Grand Forks, N.D., through floodwaters and ice slabs as the flooding Red River moves north.

NATIONAL GUARDSMEN shore up the compromised area of the flood wall on the north side of the Oak Grove campus.

DAVID SAMSON / THE FORUM

OAK GROVE PRINCIPAL
Morgan Forness looks over flood damage in the school's Benson Building.

DAVID SAMSON
THE FORUM

MICHAEL VOSBURG / THE FORUM

VERONA WINKLER hands her 10-month-old son, Cameron, to her mother, Ruth Herman, shortly after being evacuated from her home in Highland Park north of Fargo.

A LONE PEDESTRIAN makes his way across the Veterans Memorial Bridge over the Red River through a blinding snowfall.

DAVID SAMSON
THE FORUM

TUESDAY, MARCH 31

IT WASN'T JUST the floodwaters that concerned people when they woke up.

In fact, for most, it was tough to even catch a glimpse of the feisty Red through the wall of white snow – 10 inches to be exact.

There was worry about what all this snow would do to the river and a potential second crest.

But there was good news, too.

The river was retreating. It was now below 38 feet.

Better yet, some evacuated residents were returning to their homes.

DR. VIJAY GABA, a MeritCare physician, climbs a bridge over a secondary dike to return to his Rose Creek home. The neighborhood association built several such bridges for the residents.

MICHAEL VOSBURG
THE FORUM

A SHELF OF ICE REMAINS FROZEN in the trees in the Oakport
Township area as the Red River falls.

DAVE WALLIS / THE FORUM

WATER POURS from the mouth of a mounted walleye that was pulled out of Dick Knutson's flooded basement in Briarwood. The water was up to the ceiling.

CAROLYN KASTER
THE ASSOCIATED PRESS

CAROLYN KASTER / THE ASSOCIATED PRESS

ED SAMUELSON walks through knee-high water as he attempts to salvage a wet bear rug from Red River floodwaters in Dick Knutson's Briarwood basement.

WEDNESDAY, APRIL 1

ROUTINE WASN'T A WORD in many people's vocabulary at this point.

But it felt good to get back to it – even if just a little bit – after an exhausting run-in with Mother Nature.

Businesses were given the green light to reopen.

City crews began looking to fill potholes, made worse by all the truck traffic used to fight the flood.

Rural Cass County residents were going back to their flooded homes and yards.

In small cities like Briarwood, just south of Fargo, half a dozen homes were spared, while some 20 others felt the wrath of the rivers.

Cleanup would be a long road, and it was just the beginning.

NORTH DAKOTA ARMY NATIONAL GUARD TROOPS load unused Hesco Bastion barricades onto a Hemmit truck at Fargo's 10th Street South and River Drive for delivery to Fargo's North Dakota Air Guard base.

DAVID SAMSON
THE FORUM

A CITY TRUCK drives along Fargo's Harwood Drive with the neighborhood split by two levels of Hesco Bastion barricades as part of the city's secondary levee protection.

MICHAEL VOSBURG / THE FORUM

JOEL HOFFMAN, manager of apartments at 18 4th St. N. in Moorhead, removes sandbags protecting the building's front entrance.

MICHAEL VOSBURG
THE FORUM

THURSDAY, APRIL 2

THE COST OF CLEANING up after the flood was bound to be high.

The "Spirit of Fargo Flood Fund" would surely help. City officials also got word that the Federal Emergency Management Agency would reimburse the North Dakota National Guard and Fargo more than $1.3 billion for costs incurred during the flood.

It was helpful to know, but it wouldn't be an immediate relief for those still battling water.

Take the area south of Harwood, for example. Floodwaters submerged the roads there connecting 40 or 50 residents to the outside world.

Families had to ferry from homes to school and work.

HANA DUBINOVIC wheels in Bethany Homes resident Lilly Flaten to cheers. Residents had been evacuated as a precaution.

DAVID SAMSON
THE FORUM

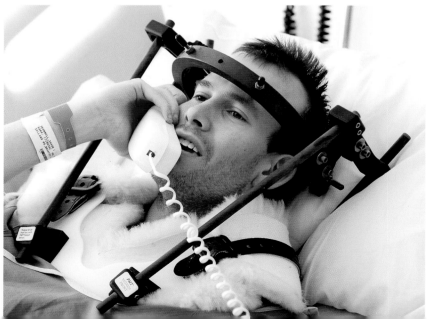

SHAWN O'DONNELL talks with a friend and former EVAC volunteer who called from Alaska to see how he was doing. The Fargo EVAC worker was directing flood-related traffic when he was hit by a car. He has been healing and going through therapy at Innovis Health.

HOPING, WAITING, PRAYING

FRIDAY, APRIL 3

THE NEWS CAME LIKE A PUNCH
TO THE GUT: The Red River would have a second crest
that could be as bad or worse than what residents had just lived
through.

It couldn't be.

Fargo Mayor Dennis Walaker declared it wouldn't be.

He dismissed the new National Weather Service data and scolded the
agency for releasing such a gloom-and-doom prediction on a Friday.

What people really needed, he said, was a relaxing weekend.

And so residents went on with their lives, buoyed by Walaker's
words but still worried.

What if the weather service was right?

**NORTH DAKOTA
GOV. JOHN
HOEVEN,**
right, and Minnesota
Gov. Tim Pawlenty
address the need for
permanent flood
protection for the Red
River Valley.

CARRIE SNYDER
THE FORUM

MARY, 8, AND KELLY NOAH, 10, look for customers at their lemonade stand along Eighth Street in south Fargo. The sisters thought it would be a good idea to raise money for flood relief on their day off from school. They raised $1,000, which was matched by the Impact Foundation for another $1,000.

METANOIA, from Sts. Anne and Joachim
Catholic Church, performs during "The Crest:
Community Prayer and Praise Gathering" at
the Fargo Theatre.

MICHAEL VOSBURG / THE FORUM

SATURDAY & SUNDAY APRIL 4-5

THE WEEKEND would be for resting and rejuvenating – just as Mayor Walaker asked – but it was hard not to dwell on that impending second crest.

City leaders asked residents to begin inspecting their own dikes and counting unused sandbags. Meanwhile, FEMA teams were doing their own inspections, touring damaged areas of Clay, Cass and Richland counties.

Flood-fighting efforts picked up again in Fargo and Moorhead on Sunday, as city workers began building contingency dikes in vulnerable areas.

It was hard to imagine the river rising again. After all, it was falling at a rate of just under half a foot a day and was now down to 34 feet.

BILL BELANGER, senior vice president of the Waterford at Harwood Groves, greets resident Marcy Fellbaum as she returns to the facility. Nearly all of the Waterford's 130 residents were back home after being evacuated March 25 and 26.

SHERRI RICHARDS
THE FORUM

MONDAY, APRIL 6

IT WAS TIME to get back at it.

Fargo and Moorhead began raising existing levees and building more backup dikes. Residents of Oxbow, N.D., rallied around fellow neighbors to help keep out the second round of water.

For the most part, though, things were less intense this time around because so much work had been done ahead of the first crest.

Students returned to classes as planned, and much of the city was attempting to get back to normal despite the looming threat of the second crest.

STEVE HAUGE collects garbage along his route in north Fargo as services resumed after being suspended during the flood fight.

DAVID SAMSON
THE FORUM

FARGO POLICE officer Sara Cruze stops traffic for Jeff Hallman and his son, Kevin, 6, as they make their way to Centennial Elementary School along 25th Street in south Fargo on the first day school resumed.

DAVID SAMSON
THE FORUM

KELVIN PEDERSON packs sand in a Hesco barricade on Highway 81 northwest of Oxbow, N.D. Most of the city was surrounded by a levee in preparation for the second flood crest.

MICHAEL VOSBURG / THE FORUM

TUESDAY, APRIL 7

A COLLECTION
of spare sandbags is piled in front of the Grand Mason Lodge along 14th Avenue North in Fargo.

DAVID SAMSON
THE FORUM

THIS TIME the revised weather service prediction came with a collective sigh of relief.

The river would likely peak at 38 to 40 feet between April 16 and 18. While still considered a massive flood at either stage, the cities' dikes and levees had just held up to a similar test and were built to handle it.

Still, there would be one last sandbagging push to go even higher, just to be safe.

AUDREY JOHNSON
looks over the water-filled dike running through her neighborhood along Ninth Street North in Moorhead. The city announced it would replace these dikes with clay sometime that week.

DAVID SAMSON
THE FORUM

WEDNESDAY, APRIL 8

MOORHEAD NEEDED 500,000 more sandbags. Fargo figured it needed 400,000 more.

Sounded like a lot. But not when you consider volunteers had already filled more than 2 million so far, keeping the rivers mostly at bay.

In Fargo-Moorhead, there were more signs of life getting back to normal.

Oak Grove students returned to classes at Fargo South Campus II. It was an unfamiliar place, but it would be home for the rest of the school year.

DAVID SAMSON / THE FORUM

FARGO OAK GROVE STUDENTS fill their lockers and head to class on their first day at Fargo South Campus II.

THURSDAY & FRIDAY APRIL 9-10

FOR FARGO AND MOORHEAD FOLKS, there was nothing to do now but wait.

But in places like Lisbon, N.D., the fight was picking up steam. The city was marking its 18th day of flood fighting, but the Sheyenne River was still not ready to settle in its banks. By weekend's end, the river could surpass the 19.29 record crest from 1997.

Areas south of Horace, N.D., to Kindred, N.D., also were bracing for the Sheyenne's wrath.

Meanwhile, flood victims in 26 North Dakota counties and four in Minnesota got word they would be eligible for individual assistance.

MILLIE DICK of Englevale, N.D., helps fill sandbags in Lisbon with Corey Baxter of Oakes, N.D., at right.

MICHAEL VOSBURG
THE FORUM

U.S. FOREST SERVICE WORKERS, from left, Kevin McElvane of Dickinson, N.D., and Stacy Swenson of Kindred help lay a sandbag dike to protect a home in Lisbon.

MICHAEL VOSBURG
FORUM PHOTO EDITOR

A SANDBAG DIKE is built around a home along the Sheyenne River in Valley City, N.D.

MICHAEL VOSBURG
THE FORUM

MARK VOXLAND

MAYOR, MOORHEAD

BY DAVE OLSON / THE FORUM

DAVID SAMSON/THE FORUM

MOORHEAD resident Paul Hilleren talked about losing his southside home to the flood. Moorhead Mayor Mark Voxland listened.

And on that day – during the height of the 2009 spring flood – Voxland got an earful.

The Moorhead resident explained how he should have trusted his gut and stayed with his home. When he left, the pumps were still staying ahead of water seeping through the dike around his home on Elm Street. But then the National Guard showed up and gave him and his neighbors a talking-to.

"Everything was the worst-case scenario."

So Hilleren left. When he called the number evacuees were supposed to call, his power was shut off. Then went the pumps. And there went his basement. The man's anger wasn't entirely directed at Voxland that day, but toward the city.

"I still like my mayor. I truly think he's got a lot on his plate," Hilleren said.

Similar sentiments were expressed during City Council meetings during the flood fight, when a number of people told officials they felt the city ignored calls for help.

Council members, including Voxland, didn't challenge the comments.

Instead, he listened.

Voxland, who was elected mayor in 2001 and won re-election four years later, said he was aware some Moorhead residents felt Fargo got more media attention during the flood, and he said at times that probably was the case.

In the buildup to the crest, Fargo and Cass County officials held televised meetings at 8 a.m. every day, which were often attended by members of the national and international media.

"We were doing a 4 o'clock press conference those first several days," Voxland said. "We figured out that was a poor time to do it, because electronic media needed to be on the air at 5 o'clock and didn't have time to do a story. We lost because of that."

While Fargo Mayor Dennis Walaker became somewhat of a national celebrity for his no-nonsense approach to flood-fighting, the 58-year-old Voxland kept a lower profile.

Voxland said he doesn't see himself as Moorhead's champion flood-fighter, stating that distinction belongs to City Engineer Bob Zimmerman.

"He (Zimmerman) has probably been the general," Voxland said, adding that the city engineer does a good job of quickly forming new defenses in the face of an ever-changing enemy.

But Bill Schwandt, general manager of Moorhead Public Service, said Voxland spent plenty of time on the front lines.

"At the peak of the intensity, in the basement of the emergency operations center when we'd go from 7 in the morning to 1 in the morning, he (Voxland) was there at all those important meetings," Schwandt said.

"He listens a lot and then, when it's time for something to be said, he's prepared to say it," Schwandt said of Voxland.

But words have a way of sometimes coming back to haunt.

During his State of the City address in early March 2009, Voxland joked that Moorhead's flood plan was to use Fargo as a retention pond. The remark drew laughs from the audience.

Voxland said the comment was a friendly jab at Walaker, and he said it was made at a time when 37 feet was considered major flooding.

"At that moment, with that group, it was a good thing to say," Voxland said. "With the flood at this level, it doesn't have a ring of humor with it. At 41 feet, we're all a retention pond."

Between his duties as mayor and working at his family's electrical contracting business, Voxland said he never hit a wall during the flood fight. But he said he was discouraged at times by ever-rising crest predictions. He cited a news conference where the city announced it was prepared for a 42-foot crest.

As the briefing wrapped up, a whisper began that the National Weather Service had changed its forecast to include the possibility of a 43-foot crest.

"All of a sudden everybody's phone rang at the same time. It was like, 'Ah, rats. It's true,'"

Voxland said.

"I went home that night, and I felt, 'How can we beat this flood, when every day they raise the crest a foot?'

"What got me out of it was the next day. I got into a line with some people and sandbagged for a couple of hours," said Voxland.

All of them, he said, had the attitude of: " 'They raised it a foot. Let's get this thing done.' It was the shot in the arm I needed."

Another emotional moment for Voxland came during a chapel service at Concordia College following the first crest. The mayor choked up a bit when students applauded him as he stepped to the altar to address the student body.

"I'm the one who's supposed to applaud all of you," Voxland said. "The words are so inadequate for what you all did, but thank you, thank you very much."

SPRING 2009

CHAPTER 4: SHEYENNE'S FURY

THE ANTIQUE WALKING BRIDGE,
a landmark in Valley City, is closed as the
Sheyenne River rises.

CARRIE SNYDER / THE FORUM

SATURDAY, APRIL 11

ALL EYES SHIFTED toward Valley City, N.D., a city of 6,800 people prepared for the challenge of a lifetime.

The National Weather Service was predicting the Sheyenne River to rise to 22 feet by Tuesday – 2 feet higher than the record set in 1882.

New river charts had to be made because the prediction was off the charts.

Bridges were closed, and National Guard soldiers patrolled the town.

STEVE SHIRLEY, president of Valley City State University, walks along one of the dikes running through campus.

CARRIE SNYDER
THE FORUM

SUNDAY, APRIL 12

IT WAS EASTER SUNDAY, but there wasn't a lot to rejoice about for residents of Valley City and rural Cass County.

In the Willow Creek subdivision west of West Fargo, neighbors were preparing to be deluged from both the Sheyenne and Maple rivers.

Cass County Road 17 had water flowing over it north of West Fargo.

This flood just didn't seem to be letting up, and residents were growing weary.

SUMP PUMPS work steadily at Kevin McCarvel's home just outside of Kindred.

CARRIE SNYDER
THE FORUM

DEB REYNOLDS, clockwise from top, Angie Michaelsohn and Fern Sessing fill sandbags outside the Michaelsohn residence in the Willow Creek subdivision west of West Fargo. They estimated about 10,000 sandbags were made over the weekend.

CARRIE SNYDER
THE FORUM

SHEYENNE'S FURY

MONDAY, APRIL 13

THE SHEYENNE continued to be the problem river and was putting immense strain on levees all along its path. A breach in one near the Valley City State University campus prompted the city to evacuate slightly less than one-third of the city.

Water also prompted officials to close Interstate 94 between Bismarck and Jamestown.

Cass County residents had to drive with caution because roads in the west and southwest were either damaged or submerged in water.

Meanwhile, the Red in Fargo-Moorhead continued to retreat and was now at 32.51 feet.

THE SHEYENNE RIVER reaches the bottom of the Rainbow Bridge on the east side of Valley City.

DAVID SAMSON
THE FORUM

CHRISTIAN DISASTER RELIEF members made up of volunteers from the Mennonite communities of Park River, N.D., and Watertown, S.D., fill sandbags at the Valley City Winter Show building.

DAVID SAMSON / THE FORUM

MOTORISTS WEAVE their way through piles of sand covering the storm drain covers in downtown Valley City.

DAVID SAMSON
THE FORUM

WILL OVER WATER 95

A RED X is placed on the door by Brenden Pollert as he evacuates the Open Door Children's Program group home in Valley City under the voluntary evacuation of that part of the city. Red Xs marked property that had been left behind.

DAVE WALLIS / THE FORUM

TUESDAY, APRIL 14

A RED X MARKED the doors of those who fled their Valley City homes after Valley City Mayor Mary Lee Nielson asked all those living in the city's flood plain and all vulnerable populations to evacuate – about half the city.

With fewer people, there would be less pressure on the city's water and sewer systems.

More Guard soldiers arrived to assist with the evacuations.

To the south, in Lisbon, the call went out for more sandbaggers.

Even places like LaMoure, N.D., were asking people along the low-lying James River to leave, and no-travel advisories were issued.

SANDY SCHEIDEGGER pulls her boat in after rowing across the water-filled ditch in front of her home along Cass 17 north of West Fargo.

DAVID SAMSON
THE FORUM

THE WALKING BRIDGE to Valley City State
University is flooded by the Sheyenne River.

DAVE WALLIS / THE FORUM

SHEYENNE'S FURY

WEDNESDAY, APRIL 15

FARGO-MOORHEAD RESIDENTS

were thankful to hear that the Red's second crest would now top out at 35.5 feet – several feet less than predicted.

But for those affected by the Sheyenne and Maple rivers, it didn't matter. Overland flooding was already upon them.

Near the small town of Kathryn, N.D., workers rushed to repair the eroding Clausen Springs Dam. National Guard members used Blackhawk helicopters to drop two dozen 1,000-pound sandbags on a corner of the dam to divert water from the dam's emergency spillway.

It was a mess, and Kathryn residents had little choice but to pack up their belongings and head to safer ground.

Jack Velure, right, who lives nearby, talks with people on the other side of a huge washout of a country road with two large culverts west of Kathryn.

DAVE WALLIS / THE FORUM

CATTLE ARE STRANDED on an island created by floodwaters of the James River near Dickey, N.D. State and federal officials estimated that 91,000 cattle died from the record snowfall and flooding.

JOHN M. STEINER / THE JAMESTOWN SUN

The stars of a U.S. flag and North Dakota
National Guard trucks are seen reflected in the
window of an evacuated building in Kathryn.

DAVE WALLIS / THE FORUM

A NORTH DAKOTA Air National Guard Blackhawk helicopter positions two 1-ton sandbags at the edge of the Clausen Springs Dam and the emergency spillway as others watch. Water flowing down the spillway was quickly eroding the section of the dam at right.

DAVE WALLIS / THE FORUM

A NORTH DAKOTA AIR NATIONAL GUARD HELICOPTER carries six 1-ton sandbags to the edge of the Clausen Springs Dam as an attempt was made to control the erosion of the emergency spillway. The dam is west of Kathryn, which was evacuated due to the threat.

DAVE WALLIS / THE FORUM

NORTH DAKOTA NATIONAL GUARDSMAN ERIC JOHNSON
records video of the scene near the community hall in Kathryn as water
rises on the west side of the town. The town was almost empty except
for the soldiers.

DAVE WALLIS / THE FORUM

SHEYENNE'S FURY

JIM HOCK leaves the flooded farmhouse belonging to his parents, Don and Marilyn Hock, while checking on the property southeast of Lisbon.

DAVID SAMSON / THE FORUM

THURSDAY, APRIL 16

T H E   S H E Y E N N E still was on its war path, and residents throughout the region continued to wage battles with it.

The unruly waters caused a crack in a clay levee in Lisbon, forcing more evacuations.

In Valley City, the mayor warned that the city was still in peril, though the Sheyenne had likely crested there earlier in the week.

In Jamestown, residents began sandbagging in preparation for increased releases of water from the Jamestown and Pipestem dams.

And in Davenport, N.D., plans got under way for a clay levee. Those living there would be the next victims of overland flooding.

CATTLE EAT on high ground surrounded by floodwaters on the Jim Hock farmstead southeast of Lisbon.

DAVID SAMSON
THE FORUM

"IT'S LIKE A DEATH … YOU NEVER THINK IT'S GOING TO HAPPEN TO YOU."
– LISBON RESIDENT BETTY ANN TUFTY ON FLOODING

SPRING 2009

CHAPTER 5

THE ROAD TO NORMAL

THE SHEYENNE DIVERSION winds
between flooded farmland on the right and
West Fargo on the left as seen looking
southeast from Interstate 94.

MICHAEL VOSBURG / THE FORUM

FRIDAY-SUNDAY
APRIL 17-19

JUST WHEN THINGS seemed to be calming down in Valley City, a sewer failure – caused by pressure from the still-flooded Sheyenne – forced more evacuations.

The city now had to run its sewage into the river, which meant the sewer system was off limits. People who remained would have to make use of the more than 200 portable toilets the city was rushing in.

It was a huge blow to people's psyches. Just a few days earlier there was hope of life getting back to normal.

But if there's anything we had learned about flooding, it's that it's unpredictable.

Life had turned into a waiting game for people in communities like Kindred and Davenport.

The Sheyenne already was breaking out of its banks south of Kindred, where water forced its way over State Highway 46 with such force that a culvert collapsed and forced the state Department of Transportation to close a major section of it.

At the same time, part of the James River bank was in need of shoring up after a tree fell in the water.

Things were more stable now, but uncertainty still loomed.

THE SHEYENNE RIVER had flooded much of the land around the
Highline Bridge in Valley City.

MICHAEL VOSBURG / THE FORUM

COLLIN WALTH, right, and Rodney Campbell unload a portable toilet in downtown Valley City. Spiffy Biffs planned to place about 500 units around the town.

CARRIE SNYDER
THE FORUM

DAVID SAMSON/THE FORUM

CASS COUNTY SHERIFF PAUL LANEY monitors activity at the Tactical Operations Center housed at the West Fargo Police Department.

MONDAY & TUESDAY APRIL 20-21

LIFE WAS STILL not back to normal in Valley City.

Businesses and schools were still shut down. The city would still be without a sewer system for a few more days.

The Sheyenne was still at a historic high – 19.7 feet. It was just below the previous record of 20 feet in 1882.

But in Fargo-Moorhead, the worst seemed to be over, and talk had shifted to cleanup.

The dikes were coming down.

It was almost hard to imagine a city without sandbag walls, but it would be a welcome change.

LOCAL LANDOWNER RAYMOND NORGARD installs fence posts next to a gravel road under water southeast of Kindred so he and other residents can safely drive over it.

MICHAEL VOSBURG
THE FORUM

SANDBAGS ARE PILED UP for collection along Wall Street in north Moorhead as Cargill volunteers, from left, Davis Thompson, Dan Simmons and Ryan Jorgensen help Oakport residents Jarrett and Joe Jenni dispose of the trailer load.

DAVID SAMSON / THE FORUM

THE PAVEMENT on Highway 46 collapsed two miles southwest of Kindred after the culvert underneath it was flushed out from under the road.

MICHAEL VOSBURG
THE FORUM

A LOADER scoops up sandbags that have been hauled from Fargo and Cass County to dump them into the shredder at left at the Cass County Highway Department in West Fargo. The long side-dump trucks, which carry about 20 tons of sandbags in each load, were bringing them in faster than the shredder could handle, causing the huge pile in the background. About 6 million sandbags were collected in Cass County. Moorhead's bags were processed in Moorhead.

DAVE WALLIS / THE FORUM

CLEANING UP

IT HAD BEEN A LONG MONTH.

Between the weather and the flood, people were worn out. At the same time, they were feeling good.

By now it seemed safe to say the region had largely won the war against the spring 2009 flood, despite losing a few battles along the way. And we had done it together.

But there was still a long road ahead.

Cleanup.

Buyouts.

Permanent flood control.

All were on the horizon. All will be at the forefront of our minds for months and years to come.

A BOBCAT scoops up a load of sandbag remains after they came out of a shredder Tuesday at the Cass County Highway Department in West Fargo. Behind the Bobcat is some of the sand that has already been removed from a portion of the six million sandbags that are being collected from Fargo and Cass County that were used in the flood-fighting efforts. The sand will be used for fill and construction and the bags will go to a landfill.

DAVE WALLIS
THE FORUM

EPILOGUE

THE FLOOD IS OVER, but its effects still linger throughout the greater Red River Valley.

Whether you live in Fargo-Moorhead, Valley City, Grand Forks or Wahpeton-Breckenridge, you likely were impacted in some way.

The one thing we all have in common: a sense of pride in the spirit of the people who rallied together to save the cities.

There were countless sleepless nights along the way. Volunteers logged thousands of hours huddled in the cold, helping to build a line of defense that would ultimately keep us out of harm's way.

Without those people, we might not have been so successful.

Spirit of youth. Pride of community. Will over water.

It was these things that helped us fight the flood of 2009.

PUBLIC OFFICIALS from local, state and federal offices from North Dakota and Minnesota gather for a historic meeting May 5 in the Capitol in Washington to confront flooding in the Red River Valley.

MICHAEL VOSBURG
THE FORUM

ACKNOWLEDGMENTS

WHILE VOLUNTEERS lined neighborhoods to help fight the flood, The Forum's reporters and photographers hit the streets to cover it. Long days and sleepless nights were the norm, but the result was comprehensive and unmatched daily coverage of the spring 2009 flood. A special thank you to all of The Forum staff members. This book would not have been possible without all of their hard work and reporting during the flood. Also thank you to Forum General Manager James Boberg, Circulation Director Curt Christensen and the following Forum employees who had a hand in this book: Paul Evenson, Jill Colosky, Alyssa Wiedenmeyer, Stephanie Selensky and Dianna Baumann.

SAYWARD HONER / THE FORUM

THE FORUM'S FLOOD COVERAGE TEAM

Front row, from left to right: Tracy Frank, Amy Dalrymple, Kelly Smith, Tammy Swift, Stephanie Selensky, Kathy Tofflemire, Angie Wieck. **Second row, from left to right:** Mila Koumpilova, Jeff Kolpack, Carrie Snyder, Sherri Richards, Brittany Lawonn, Michael Vosburg, Jon Knutson, Dave Wallis, Meredith Holt **Third row, from left to right:** Mary Jo Hotzler, Hayden Goethe, Rob Beer, Jay Ulku, Neil Mulka, Steve Wagner, Shane Mercer **Fourth row, from left to right:** Patrick Springer, Dave Roepke, Robert Morast, Dave Olson, Heath Hotzler, Matthew Von Pinnon, Devlyn Brooks **Fifth row, from left to right:** Tom Mix, Troy Becker, Kevin Schnepf, Mike Nowatzki, Dianna Baumann, Craig McEwen, Eric Peterson, Dan Haglund **Not pictured:** Helmut Schmidt, John Lamb, Kerry Collins, David Samson, Jason Miller, Jack Zaleski, Ryan Babb, Lonna Whiting, Mark Merck

FLOOD BOOK ACKNOWLEDGMENTS
Editor: Mary Jo Hotzler
Designer: Neil Mulka
Photo editor: Michael Vosburg
Coordinator: Matthew Von Pinnon

HOW THE RIVERS ROSE

GRAPHICS BY TROY BECKER
THE FORUM

THE RED RIVER AT FARGO-MOORHEAD

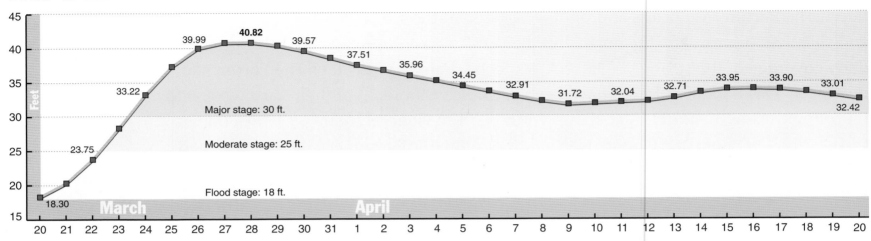

THE SHEYENNE RIVER AT VALLEY CITY, ND

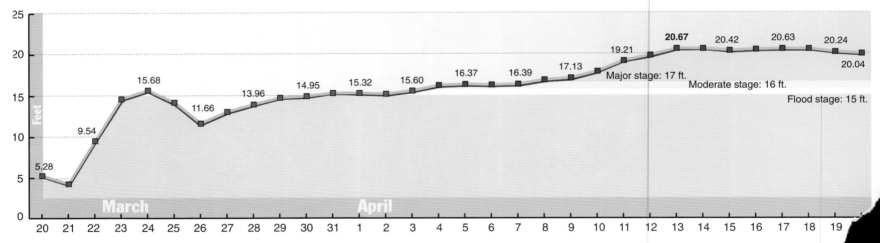

THE WILD RICE RIVER AT ABERCROMBIE, ND

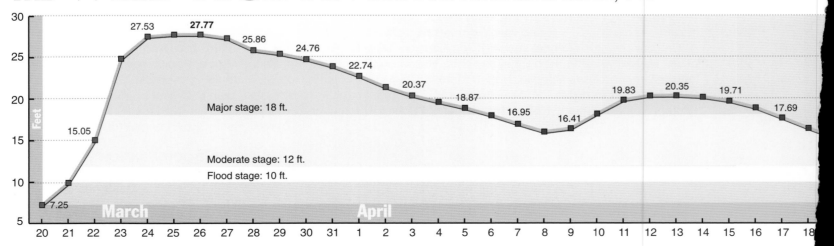

RIVER CREST

40.82 FT.

DATE OF CREST: MARCH 28

FLOOD WATERS
of the Red River
engulf Moorhead
homes near
Woodlawn Park.

MICHAEL VOSBURG
THE FORUM

RIVER CREST

20.67 FT.

DATE OF CREST: APRIL 13

A FARM
sits under water
from the flooded
Sheyenne River
near Valley City.

MICHAEL VOSBURG
THE FORUM

RIVER CREST

27.77 FT.

DATE OF CREST: MARCH 26

KE WIESER
he grounds of
ed farmstead
he Wild Rice
River.

DAVID SAMSON
THE FORUM

FORUM FLOOD FRONTS

SUNDAY, MARCH 22

MONDAY, MARCH 23

TUESDAY, MARCH 24

WEDNESDAY, MARCH 25

UNCHARTED TERRITORY

THURSDAY, MARCH 26

FIGHT OR FLIGHT

FRIDAY, MARCH 27

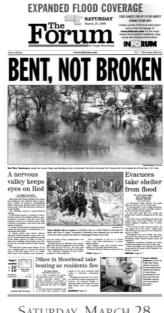

BENT, NOT BROKEN

SATURDAY, MARCH 28

HOLDING STEADY

SUNDAY, MARCH 29

Buoyed by faith

MONDAY, MARCH 30

A cold blast of

TUESDAY, MAR